Time Goes By

A Year in the World of Dinosaurs

Elizabeth Havercroft

M Millbrook Press / Minneapolis

First American edition published in 2009 by Lerner Publishing Group, Inc.

Copyright © 2008 by Orpheus Books Ltd.

Millbrook Press
A division of Lerner Publishing Group, Inc.
241 First Avenue North
Minneapolis, MN 55401 USA

Website address: www.lernerbooks.com

The publisher wishes to thank scientific consultant Professor Michael Benton, Department of Earth Sciences, University of Bristol, Bristol, England

Library of Congress Cataloging-in-Publication Data

Havercroft, Elizabeth.
    A year in the world of dinosaurs / by Elizabeth Havercroft. — 1st American ed.
        p.   cm. -- (Time goes by)
    Includes index.
    ISBN 978-1-58013-548-1 (lib. bdg. : alk. paper)
    1. Paleontology—Jurassic—Juvenile literature. 2. Dinosaurs—Juvenile literature. 3. Year—Juvenile literature. 4. Months—Juvenile literature. I. Title.
    QE733.H38 2009
    567.9—dc22   2007039036

Manufactured in the United States of America
1 2 3 4 5 6 – BP – 14 13 12 11 10 09

Table of Contents

THIS IS THE STORY of a year in the lives of some dinosaurs. All the pictures have the same view. But each one shows a different time of year. Lots of things happen during this year. Can you spot them all?

This story takes place during the Jurassic period. This period was about 150 million years ago. All the dinosaurs in this book lived in North America during this time.

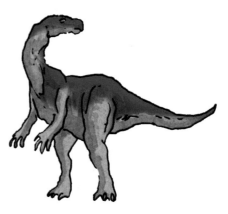

You can follow all the action as the months pass. The calendar on each right-hand page tells you which month you've reached.

Some dinosaurs appear on every page. Look out for the four young adult *Diplodocus*. They have spikes down their back. Watch the *Diplodocus* baby as it grows up. This book has lots of prehistoric creatures to spot!

As you read, imagine what a dinosaur scientist would notice each month. Think about what stories the scientist might tell about life in the Jurassic period.

Can you
find . . .

Diplodocus?

It is early morning on the plain. *Diplodocus* babies are hatching. They are in danger. A pack of hungry *Ornitholestes* is nearby. They have dark stripes across their backs. The four *Diplodocus* young adults do not watch the babies. They drink water from the river.

April

Babies hatch

Torvosaurus attack

Forest fire

Burned land

Floods

Mating season

Making nests

Moving on

Can you
find . . .

Ceratosaurus?

Barosaurus?

The weather is hotter and drier this month. The trees are starting to wilt. A hungry *Torvosaurus* goes on the attack. *Stegosaurus* protects itself with its spiky tail. The *Diplodocus* youngsters watch from a safe distance. *Ceratosaurus* catches fish. But a crocodile watches nearby. Far off, a herd of *Barosaurus* arrives on the plain. The herd is looking for food.

June

Babies hatch

***Torvosaurus* attack**

Forest fire

Burned land

Floods

Mating season

Making nests

Moving on

Can you
find . . .

Stegosaurus?

a flying reptile?

The weather is very dry and hot. A forest fire has broken out. The fire scares the dinosaurs. Some start running. The sounds of galloping feet fill the air. A mother looks back to check that her baby is safe. Flying reptiles soar above the trees to escape the flames. *Stegosaurus* must hurry so that the fire does not catch it.

August

Babies hatch

Torvosaurus attack

Forest fire

Burned land

Floods

Mating season

Making nests

Moving on

Can you
find . . .

Allosaurus?

a mammal?

some bones?

The fire has finally ended. All the plants and trees are badly burned. The riverbed is dry. The dinosaurs have no food or water. A pack of *Allosaurus* attacks an old and frightened *Diplodocus*. Some tiny mammals watch. The *Diplodocus* young adults run away.

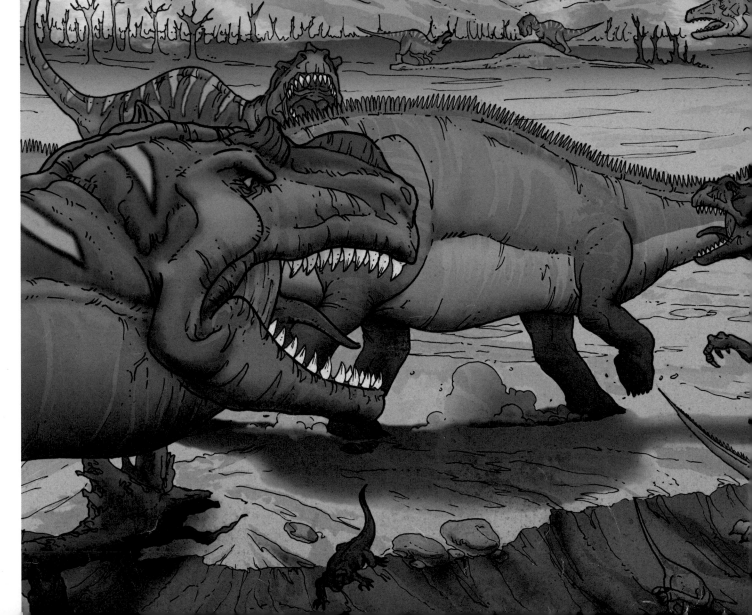

September

Babies hatch

Torvosaurus attack

Forest fire

Burned land

Floods

Mating season

Making nests

Moving on

Can you
find . . .

a plesiosaur?

a crocodile?

Ichthyosaurus?

a fish?

The rainy season has started. The river begins to flood. Some reptiles arrive from the sea. The flood gave them a way to swim to this area. Plesiosaurs lift their long necks out of the water. Flying reptiles swoop down to catch fish. Two *Diplodocus* babies play on an island. Two crocodiles swim toward them.

14

November

Babies hatch

Torvosaurus attack

Forest fire

Burned land

Floods

Mating season

Making nests

Moving on

Can you
find . . .

Camarasaurus?

Dryosaurus?

Dimorphodon?

a palm tree?

The floodwaters have gone down. Male and female dinosaurs are ready to mate to make baby dinosaurs. The *Diplodocus* males put on a display. They stamp, snort, and whip their tails to get the females' attention. The females don't seem to notice! A huge *Camarasaurus* watches them while it eats.

December

Babies hatch

Torvosaurus attack

Forest fire

Burned land

Floods

Mating season

Making nests

Moving on

Can you
find . . .

a dinosaur egg?

a nest?

Tanycolagreus?

Anurognathus?

The plain is green once more. The *Diplodocus* females are making their nests. They build mounds of soil with their teeth. Then they lay their eggs in the nests. They don't guard the nests very well. Small dinosaurs steal some of the eggs.

January

Babies hatch

Torvosaurus attack

Forest fire

Burned land

Floods

Mating season

Making nests

Moving on

Can you
find . . .

Coelurus?

Camptosaurus?

Pterodactylus?

a lizard?

ferns?

a volcano?

Diplodocus must move to new feeding grounds. The herd travels together. Just one baby has survived since being born last April. It joins the herd, along with the four young adults. A few flying reptiles ride on the backs of *Diplodocus*. Some *Coelurus* and *Camptosaurus* stay behind to see what the next season brings.

March

Babies hatch

Torvosaurus attack

Forest fire

Burned land

Floods

Mating season

Making nests

Moving on

Pronunciation Guide

Allosaurus (AL-uh-SAWR-uhs)

Anurognathus (an-YOOR-og-nath-uhs)

Barosaurus (BAR-uh-SAWR-uhs)

Camarasaurus (CAM-uh-ruh-SAWR-uhs)

Camptosaurus (CAMP-tuh-SAWR-uhs)

Ceratosaurus (suh-RAT-uh-SAWR-uhs)

Coelurus (sih-LUR-uhs)

Dimorphodon (die-MOOR-fuh-don)

Diplodocus (dih-PLAH-dih-kuhs)

Dryosaurus (DRY-uh-SAWR-uhs)

Ichthyosaurus (IHK-thee-uh-SAWR-uhs)

Ornitholestes (or-NITH-uh-LEHS-tees)

plesiosaurs (PLEE-zee-uh-SAWRZ)

Pterodactylus (TAIR-uh-DAK-tih-luhs)

Stegosaurus (STEHG-uh-SAWR-uhs)

Tanycolagreus (tan-EE-koh-LAG-ree-uhs)

Torvosaurus (TOR-vuh-SAWR-uhs)

Glossary

fern: a plant with featherlike leaves and no flowers

mammals: warm-blooded animals that have backbones, breathe air, and produce milk for their young

mate: to make baby animals

reptiles: cold-blooded animals that have backbones and scaly skin, breathe air, and lay eggs

wilt: when a plant droops because it does not have enough water

Learn More about Dinosaurs

Books

Holtz, Thomas R. *Dinosaurs: The Most Complete, Up-to-Date Encyclopedia for Dinosaur Lovers of All Ages*. New York: Random House, 2007.

Hort, Lenny. *Did Dinosaurs Eat Pizza?: Mysteries Science Hasn't Solved*. New York: Henry Holt and Co., 2006.

Lessem, Don. *Sea Giants of Dinosaur Time*. Minneapolis: Millbrook Press, 2005.

Long, John. *Dinosaurs*. New York: Simon and Schuster Books for Young Readers, 2007.

Sheldon, David. *Barnum Brown: Dinosaur Hunter*. New York: Walker & Co., 2006.

Walker, Sally M. *The Search for Antarctic Dinosaurs*. Minneapolis: Millbrook Press, 2008.

Wheeler, Lisa. *Dino-hockey*. Minneapolis: Carolrhoda Books, 2007.

Websites

Dinosaur Bones

http://www.abc.net.au/dinosaurs/dino_playground/games/bones/default.htm

In this online game, you must put the dinosaur bones together correctly.

Paleontology and Geology Glossary

http://www.enchantedlearning.com/subjects/dinosaurs/glossary/

Part of the Enchanted Learning website, this glossary gives the meaning of dinosaur names as well as physical descriptions. It also includes links to more information.

Sue at the Field Museum

http://www.fieldmuseum.org/sue/index.html

Learn all about Sue, the largest, most complete, and best preserved *Tyrannosaurus rex* fossil.

A Closer Look

This book has a lot to find. Did you imagine you were a scientist as you read? Some scientists study dinosaurs and other life-forms from long ago. They are called paleontologists. All kinds of scientists keep notebooks for writing down their ideas and the things they notice.

Pretend you are a paleontologist. You will need a piece of paper and a pencil. The paper will be your scientific notebook. Write the name of the month at the top of the page. Underneath, write about what the dinosaurs are doing during that month. What do they do all day long? Are they facing any dangers? What? Have you seen anything surprising? What? What do you hope to see next month?

Don't worry if you don't know how to spell every word. You can ask a parent or teacher for help if you need to. And be creative!

Index